Catena Poetica

An International Collaboration

poems by

**Flor Aguilera,
Joyce Brinkman,
Gabriele Glang,**
and **Carolyn Kreiter-Foronda**

Finishing Line Press
Georgetown, Kentucky

Catena Poetica

An International Collaboration

Copyright ©2022 by Flor Aguilera, Joyce Brinkman, Gabriele Glang, and Carolyn Kreiter-Foronda
ISBN 978-1-64662-741-7 First Edition
All rights reserved under International and Pan-American Copyright Conventions. No part of this book may be reproduced in any manner whatsoever without written permission from the publisher, except in the case of brief quotations embodied in critical articles and reviews.

Publisher: Leah Huete de Maines
Editor: Christen Kincaid
Cover Art: Carolyn Kreiter-Foronda
Author Photos: Flor Aguilera García, Jim Martin, Janis Harless, Carl Van Dorn
Cover Design: Elizabeth Maines McCleavy

Order online: www.finishinglinepress.com
also available on amazon.com

Author inquiries and mail orders:
Finishing Line Press
PO Box 1626
Georgetown, Kentucky 40324
USA

Table of Contents

Preface

Color

Gabriele Glang, Joyce Brinkman, Carolyn Kreiter-Foronda 1

Spice

Joyce Brinkman, Flor Aguilera, Carolyn Kreiter-Foronda 6

Music

Carolyn Kreiter-Foronda, Gabriele Glang, Joyce Brinkman 11

Water

Joyce Brinkman, Carolyn Kreiter-Foronda, Flor Aguilera 16

Clouds

Gabriele Glang, Joyce Brinkman, Carolyn Kreiter-Foronda 21

Preface

This chapbook introduces a new collaborative poetry form. The idea for the form was initiated by Mexican poet Flor Aguilera, who introduced the form to her United States collaborative-writing partners Joyce Brinkman and Carolyn Kreiter-Foronda. The three poets had worked together previously with writers from Japan, Germany, and France to produce *Seasons of Sharing* (Leapfrog Press, ©2014), a book of modified kasen renku verse.

The chapbook *Catena Poetica* uses a narrative approach and relies on linking words. Three poets in rotation wrote separate and distinct narratives based on the chosen theme for each poem. The first poet set up the theme in two tercets followed by a couplet, addressed the theme broadly, and cited a mythological creature or god. The initial poet also chose and italicized eleven words in the opening narrative. In each of the subsequent sections, the poets in turn cited one of the italicized words and created a new narrative, based on the poem's subject. The collaborative poem concludes with section twelve after all italicized words have been used. Note: The italics have been removed from the final version of each poem.

In *Catena Poetica,* the U.S. poets Brinkman and Kreiter-Foronda are joined by German-American poet Gabriele Glang, who offers readers a view of the European landscape and culture in "Color," "Music," and "Clouds." Aguilera brings the richness of Mexico's Hispanic atmosphere in "Spice" and "Water." The U.S. poets add to each poem their own Midwest and East Coast flavors.

Color
Gabriele Glang, Joyce Brinkman, Carolyn Kreiter-Foronda

The alchemy of chaos: creation
began with darkness, churning. A swordslash:
light sundered sea and sky. Limning that line,

First Dawn bled into earth. The glow's embrace
suffused the blushing vapors, parting clouds,
birthed color—an infinity of hues.

Winged goddess Iris unfurled her rainbow
ribbon, reuniting us with heaven.

*

Ancient ancestors wondered who
carried the sun. Who called it forth
from the darkness of its hiding place,

to surge in orange splendor with warming
light. Life-affirming rays gracing our fair
days with perfect roundness. Making us

sense as we squeeze juice from a circle
of orange flesh, we can taste the sun.

*

Beneath the azure aura of hummingbirds,
tread earth lightly. Allow the flutter
to permeate your soul with melodies

that cast a spell and lift into heavens
as life-giving air. Let ocean's sapphire waves
radiate serenity as the rhythmic hummers

embellish clouds with steel-blue notes
that ward off evil by emanating tranquility.

*

Brown reigns in Fasnet, season of fools, mud.
How to love it, when patches of snow crust
the sodden acres' shadowed troughs? Cold fogs

obscure the middle distance, sepias,
tired ochers, umbers, caput mortuums.
But midday's blush softly heralds solstice:

Leucojum vernum tides surge down the Alb
escarpments—Swabian harbingers of light.

*

Even gray displays shades. The alchemy
of any color always mixes ingenious
distinctions in tinge on different textures.

The settling of twilight's shadow on a window's
damask drapes, its blanketing the winter
bark of an ash tree or the way it wraps

the monument above a recently filled grave,
where interred ashes receive no light.

*

Among royalty, purple wields the scepter,
holds sway over bishops, monarchs, magistrates,
empowers suffragettes, ignites movements.

Gather amethyst crystals from Brazilian mines,
Tyrian dye from embroidered togas, lilac roses
from floral art. Refashion the world with hues

resistent to lamentation. A regal heron lifts
into flight, douses the terrain in a veil of lavender.

*

Haunted by cancer—*what if life's finite?*—
he painted helical banderoles of gold—
lemniscates—on giant, night-dark canvases.

Geometries of comfort, they evoke
his trademark stroke, the viscous twists and turns
of monochromic cityscapes. *What remains?*

A photo of a pirouetting blur
in front of gold infinities: his daughter.

*

Delight lies in the eye. It dances
in that circle which grows and shrinks.
The space that soaks in all the lines

of luminosity. A round spot appearing black
and blank. It drinks each photon's spectrum,
granting rays safe passage to inner intelligence.

An ebony dot not keeping beams for itself,
a perfect, selfless point.

*

At Fallingwater, nature imbues the spirit,
grants passion to a florid arc of sunrise,
Cherokee red blazing in the home's ironwork.

As water cascades over rocks, a benign breeze
scintillates on cantilevered decks. Jaunty cardinals,
grosbeaks, woodpeckers flap wings in harmony

with fluttering leaves, a crimson amaryllis
at the door welcoming good fortune.

*

Let us praise chaos, maligned precursor
of transitions. A ragged mizzle veils
barely greening meadows. March's Ides rack

the eaves, silencing birdsong. Wild winds roar
in bone-bare branches. Rain clouds surge, engorged
with the salty taste of ambivalence:

that yearning to be traveling—*Fernweh*—
or buried in the sofa all day long.

*

The glistening white web of a garden
spider, patches of chalky bark encircling
old trunks of a winding river's sycamores,

large frozen sheets of winter's ice and snow
all refusing to choose one complexion
over another. Each reflecting light

in its irresistible wholeness, offering up radiant
ribbons with wavelengths equally dispersed.

*

In sanctuaries, trumpet-shaped jonquils usher in
spring wealth, their birthed petal-like tepals:
sublime as patches of yellow marigolds.

In the distance the *chip, chip* of an American
goldfinch enlivens a lawn's vast sweep
down a tidal creek's banks, the heat's flair

an invitation to bask beside a daffodil bed,
each Narcissus flower: a sign of new beginnings.

*

Spice

Joyce Brinkman, Flor Aguilera, Carolyn Kreiter-Foronda

Tempted by a taste of parsley, rosemary
and thyme, a poet savored their
bouquet at a fair; packaged them

in song. Herculean echoes of herbs
mingling with musical texture,
the smells of spices sprinkled

in oil. Steeped in wine, they keep
their succulent flavors fresh.

*

Sun pours down like fairy dust
onto still-life whites and crimson greens,
market gold, our best natures.

I walk through its fields and mountains,
smells like fragrant waves of clove,
bright marshes at the edge of the street.

As you introduce me to your morning rite,
I can sense the spices that garnish your life.

*

Oak-burning fires embellish air,
call me outdoors to search meadows
for the hidden source of fragrance.

I search Hungary for succulent cuisine,
adorned with caraway and Noble Sweet paprika—
prismatic as a spectrum of deep-red light

blended into goulash, into the miracle
of folk tunes humming in the stew.

*

The kitchen has a chest for storing
teas, instilled with special flavors, sweet
among selections tingling and tart.

Its ivory lid contains a pane of glass
through which one can view ten, tiny tins
lined accordingly with names from a to z.

To sip a cup of Apple Spiced at sunrise,
a pot of Za'atar with every evening's feast.

*

The dreamer made heaven and earth,
and fresh one morning, he created man,
a crowning achievement or an afterthought.

He liked man so he gave him a gift,
named it the yellow music.
It warms the hearth on foggy nights.

Cumin clears the conscience, tires out the soul
so it can fall asleep and dream up origin stories.

*

"Let food be thy medicine," Hippocrates said.
Revere the chemical soul of ginger root.
Finely grate this perennial herb. Boil tea.

Steep for five minutes. Add honey.
Drink until the rewards cure a sore throat,
relieve inflammation. The magic's in the taste.

Drink until a bright star douses your spirit.
Gifts you with gold and myrrh.

*

A year in West Africa whet his appetite
for adventure and turned his tongue a bit
British. His speech, his eyes aroused strange

hungers in me. He served, I ate, always hoping
for more. More time than just at the table
and more ways of keeping him close.

His fondness fell on another. Now my tongue
thinks of him nibbling Grains of Paradise.

*

High hope, like a bird, echoes from above
through cloud after cloud, pink, gray, and white.
I saw our motherland.

The landing was smooth, wine and paella,
orange, bright orange firelight, heat, and smoke.
The first spark was named saffron.

Then the blue, the remains of days spent
in Spanish sunshine and museum lighting.

*

Imagine opening the tomb of Tutankhamun
and there discovering clay models of garlic bulbs,
placed to forfend evil, repel vampires.

Like Egyptians, grow accustomed
to its pungence, to its power to cure wounds,
asthma, ward off smallpox, prolong life.

Mince, add salt, sprinkle. Bow down.
Worship this highly prized spice or herb.

    *

Fortunate the fowl, the pigs of the poor.
With masters of meager means, unable
to sacrifice such precious possessions,

livestock likenesses took their place
on ghost-white Springerles. Cookies
scented with sweet, aromatic anise oil.

An infused Christmas treat instead of
meat to amuse a small German girl.

    *

Fair is beautiful and upright.
Fair is lightness and warm weather.
In this land it is just the right amount.

Tortilla maker creates maíz from stone.
Open hand a perfect measuring cup,
she adds the hint of paprika, spice, and sauce.

This dish requires generosity in plating,
a sharp tongue to withstand all the color and heat.

    *

Ascend into the heart of the Andes.
Discover Peru's culinary heritage—
a holy trinity of ají amarillo, garlic,

and red onion. Blanch chili peppers
three times until yellow becomes orange,
until the mix of flavors adds zing.

The charm's packaged in the hot tang
as you soar, like a stately condor, into sky.

*

Music
Carolyn Kreiter-Foronda, Gabriele Glang, Joyce Brinkman

Look deep into the essence of music.
Like a composer, rearrange the order
of notes until a melodious gift

breathes with rhythm and tempo,
its harmony buoyant with color
and light waiting to energize

a minuet, rondo, concerto, sonata,
vibrant with Kokopelli's heart and soul.

*

In the beginning was song: a mother's hum
leading the small one into engulfing sleep.
Or that long breath into a mute swan's neck bone,

pierced with finger holes, making bare feet dance:
hands beat a tattoo on skin, heads raised heavenward,
appeasing spirits, begging favor, rainfall.

Or the rhythmic rattle of seeds in a gourd:
Hunger Moon and war drums driving them onward.

*

Salute the composers of Christmas carols,
hymns still carrying a simple story
from thousands of years past. Events

occurring before even one musical note
was ever written down. About people
breathing long before cathedral organs

pumped air through golden pipes. Playing
as the last air leaves a mother's lungs.

*

Listen to the cadence of a mambo,
swirling through a pine tree's branches,
acrobatic squirrels—sprightly,

hip-shaking to the wind's swagger
and glitz. Sway your hips to the lively
tempo of a skittering squirrel.

Like an audacious rodent, liberate yourself.
Follow a raucous drumbeat. Scale the tree.

*

For years I ignored the piano's ghost:
my mother's silent injunctions to play.
Now arthritic hands strain for octaves,

and my eyes struggle to unravel notes.
It takes every ounce of nerve to serve
the fruits of three months' practice: Couperin's

Barricades Mysterieuses bloom, melodious,
on a centagenarian Blüthner.

*

Dance delivers the message when
white blankets the buckwheat field
discovered by the drone scout.

At the hive he moves through
from tango to minuet, plotting
the miles and directions.

Trumpeting the itinerary
with wind from whirling wings.

*

In Bolivia, an armadillo speeds by, the whoosh
of its armored shell as animated as vibrant
strings of a charango in full swing.

Who cannot join in this jubilant atmosphere
at the Virgin of Urkupiña festival?
Quechua Indians, high-spirited, fill the streets

with fist-raising and feet-stomping vibes,
awakening earth from its deep winter sleep.

*

She bends low over her cello—*Mamusiu*—
mother, muse, the river from which she drinks,
the Vistula. Her soul follows those shores,

coaxing the curved wooden body into songs
of ephemeral encounters. Eyes closed,
her belly sends birthing groans through bared teeth.

Passion's essence wings skyward—diaphanous
as dialogues—*rallentando*, and dissolves.

*

Beloved by Confucius, guqin,
your sound travels through space
on Voyager's golden disk. Prepared

to convey morality, character,
and physics to any alien species.
Yet how can such beings receive

the energized feelings expressed
without the light of Earth's moon?

*

Dive into rollicking waves of deep-sea
denizens, the dissonance of dragonfish,
squid, frilled shark: in contrast with the yin

and yang of a mermaid's cadence,
her harp-like flow. In contrast with Mondrian's
Broadway Boogie Woogie, its primary colors

harmonious, its black checkerboard lines,
exuberant, carrying you back to the surface.

*

A sudden warm spell sets the snow melting
under blindingly perfect skies. Titmouse
and chaffinch hover in the hedges. Almost

I can hear woodwinds: chiffchaff, linnet, skylark.
But it's too early. My soul's still a closed fist.
I pace ice-laced roads between soggy acres

unfurling to blackbirds' *concerto grosso*—
mud season's prelude singing me home again.

*

Sound surrounds us. Seeps into our
most private moments. The whispering
violins of wind, the ballads of birds,

the chirping of crickets, even the low
grinding of glaciers all join the chorus.
Sounds, billions of years old, heard and

unheard, hurl through light-years of space
merging into inscrutable sonatas of song.

*

Water
                Joyce Brinkman, Carolyn Kreiter-Foronda, Flor Aguilera

Water flows slowly.
Seeps below the surface
in a sluggish race to mingle in mud.

Mazu rises to the rim of rock
cliffs, then falls, plunges,
pools in chasm and crevice.

Winding its way, water
marks a persistent path.

      *

Thunderstorms race
across the bay. No goddess
wails to protect fishermen.

No red-garbed protectress
waves workboats ashore.
No lighthouse beckons.

Only a towering replica
beams its imaginary rays.

      *

Waves stir up an awesome feast.
Sand with heaven intermingles.
Meandering shore of darkness.

A winged creature swoops.
Claws cling to nightgown,
stop her fatal race to water.

Some nights there are no dreams,
only aquatic flights of fancy.

      *

Sailing above the sea,
moon's mangled light falls
upon a cerulean wave.

Sun will soon crack open
the somnolent sky.
Beams suspended in air

hold up another day
for an awakened world.

*

Adrift, impoverished
migrants aboard a rubber
dinghy, flee war—

no life vests to hold
afloat the bodies that plunge
into the icy depths,

freedom submerged
miles from a new homeland.

*

Body plummets from the cliff.
Dark skin strapped to starlight blue,
ample sky his parachute.

Thrusting over fear to freedom,
Acapulco Cannon takes sharp plunge,
yet increases his value.

In tourists' eyes, ocean is not hard water
but a pool of petals where the diver lands.

*

To life-long journeys of
following the sun, terns
emerge from eggs perched

on rim of rock, branch of tree.
Atmospheric safety secures from
human hunters eager for

feathered hats, taste of bird,
an appetizing aphrodisiac.

*

A young boy's gunshots sail
across a shallow creek,
rattle a sliding glass door,

the elderly victims, sprawled
on the floor. The rain, persistent,
pounds earth, its path

foreboding in a climate
rife with firearms.

*

Persistent bloodstream,
difficult to clean up, dry, erase on map.
Resilient inheritance of man,

unrelenting it flows and finds
mouths to feed, banks to save,
fishermen to entertain.

The river bends, too old to go straight
towards the ocean bed, to rest.

*

Amid tan desert sands, life struggles.
Any seepage from stone becomes
a stream of life-saving visions.

Rivers call people to them
like nectar calls the humming bees.
Human hives line their banks,

only to divert, dam, or desecrate
the nourishing flows so coveted.

*

A dream of freedom
from drowning in a cave
for twelve boys and a mentor,

malnourished, sluggish
from a relentless war with water.
One rescuer dies, monsoon rains

inch closer, and then a blessing—
thirteen victors pulled to safety.

*

High-rise waves for the late surfer
arrive on time after noon,
help him fulfill another flying fantasy.

After this flight he will renounce water,
hang up old riding boots,
bid farewell to friendly fins.

Waves and mermaids will call out to him,
but a faint heartbeat will drown out their song.

*

Clouds
Gabriele Glang, Joyce Brinkman, Carolyn Kreiter-Foronda

Let us praise the clouds.
Born in the troposphere,
those mutable harbingers—

defying divinations—augur both:
destruction and deliverance.
Consider Yahweh's pillar

of clouds leading his Chosen
out of Egypt, out of slavery.

*

A tall tower of black twists
around a gleaming white pillar
in an atmospheric dance.

The fragile filament disappears
as the larger, dark veil engulfs
its reflective light. Losing heat,

condensation depletes the bleak,
dimming force bringing rain.

*

Give praise to Monteverde's
cloud forest for sustaining
moisture in a canopy of trees.

Praise this habitat for housing
the endangered quetzal,
its plumage iridescent as it lifts

through a shroud of haze—
a resplendent god, shimmering.

*

Let us give thanks for rainbows
born of mother clouds' vapors
seeding our nacreous hopes,

for capricious wisps of cirrus
beyond starlings' murmurations,
for puddles mirroring a mackerel sky.

Give thanks for the silver lining
that limns the darkest cumulonimbus.

*

Caught in the slavery of weather,
a Cold Moon remains caged
by a copious carpet of clouds.

Finding no light to hunt by,
the red fox chooses to curl
securely in the winter's den.

In evening sky's matted mist
a deer mouse survives the night.

*

On blistering summer days,
bless the remaining farm lands,
a low-hanging fog shielding

corn, soybeans, wheat crops
from sweltering sun. A comfort:
the wealth of water crystals

descending over the fields,
resisting destruction.

*

Deliverance abounds in clouds.
Behold the divine artistry
of brushstrokes, how white whorls eddy

across a cerulean canvas.
Consider the lunar fog bow—
ephemeral, prismatic gem.

Observe how winter's hoarfrost sheaths
even the spider's filaments.

*

Exalt the creator of clouds,
find sanctuary in cover
whether from sun or moon.

Glide encased in lightest metal
into night's heaven. See moonlight
divulge white swirls of divine vapor.

From a hospice window watch
clouds christening the chosen day.

*

Witness a mass of tempestuous
clouds lifting, the explosive
hurricane gone to sea—

not a creature soaring above
the wreckage, no sign
of survivors defying the odds

until a beacon of light shimmers
in the rubble: a hand trembling.

*

Contemplate the mammatus
clouds clotting a creamy sky—
heavy-breasted auguries

of Indian Summer's end. All
is falling. Gravity reigns.
Chill winds hustle the last gold

from beeches. Joy—dried rhizome—
retreats into dark earth's maw.

*

While Earth lies in shadow,
from beneath land's horizon,
the sun emblazons ice clouds.

Noctilucent in nature, mesospheric
marvels molded in its summer cold,
enchantingly appear ghost-blue.

Fed by methane, perhaps leading
to Earth's encasement in ice.

*

Like a sea eagle, fly free above
Australia's Gulf of Carpentaria.
Discover the Morning Glory Cloud

spinning in air: solitary, ignited
by mutable squalls and shears.
Honor this churning, cylindrical mass.

Honor this rare stretch of harmony:
a glorious tunnel, billowing for miles.

Flor Aguilera was born in Mexico. At the age of seven, she immigrated with her family to the United States and began a journey that took her to live in seven countries and eight different cities, including Shanghai, London, and Sydney. In 2006 and 2012, she received scholarships from FONCA and CALQ for Artistic Residencies Abroad in Montreal, Quebec and the Banff Center for the Arts in Alberta, Canada. She has published six books of poetry, including *As the Audience Begs for a Ferocious Tango*, *Butoh*, and *Fifty-five Frames per Second*.

*

Joyce Brinkman, Indiana Poet Laureate 2002-2008, believes in poetry as public art. Color and light have inspired permanent public installations through collaborations with glass artists and painters, while the colors black and white figure prominently in her paintings. Her latest printed works include *Seasons of Sharing: A Kasen Renku Collaboration* with the poets of this chapbook and *Elizabeth Barrett Browning Illuminated by the Message* in the Literary Portals to Prayer Series. Joyce has received fellowships from the Mary Anderson Center for the Arts, the Vermont Studio, and the Indianapolis Arts Council.

Gabriele Glang, a bilingual German-American writer and artist, published her German poetry debut, *Göttertage*, fictional monologues of German Expressionist painter Paula Modersohn-Becker, with Klöpfer & Meyer in 2017. Her poems have appeared in magazines, anthologies, and newspapers in the U.S., the U.K., Germany, and Italy. A screenwriter and film translator, she received script funding from Baden-Württemberg's media board. She recently received a project stipend for a musical from Baden-Württemberg's ministry of science, research, and arts. She has taught creative writing in the public and private sectors, as well as at the University of Applied Sciences at Esslingen, Germany. [www.gabrieleglang.de]

*

Dr. Carolyn Kreiter-Foronda, Virginia Poet Laureate Emerita and abstract colorist painter, has coedited three anthologies and published nine books, including *The Embrace: Diego Rivera and Frida Kahlo*. Her poems appear in the U.S. and abroad in such journals as *Nimrod, Prairie Schooner, Poet Lore, Mid-American Review, World Poetry Yearbook,* and *Best of Literary Journals*. She has won numerous awards, including the Art in Literature: The Mary Lynn Kotz Award, the Ellen Anderson Award, Virginia Cultural Laureate Award, Edgar Allan Poe Poetry Award, and the Alumna of the Year Award from both George Mason University and the University of Mary Washington. [www.carolynforonda.com]

www.ingramcontent.com/pod-product-compliance
Lightning Source LLC
LaVergne TN
LVHW041515070426
835507LV00012B/1587